Table of Contents

Rourke
Educational Media

A Division of
Carson
Dellosa
Education

rourkeeducationalmedia.com

Can you find these words?

owner

puppies

sit

toys

What do Poodle
puppies look like?

4

They have curly hair.

They get big. They grow taller than 15 inches (38 centimeters).

What do Poodle
puppies act like?

8

toy

They have lots of energy.
They play with **toys**.

They are smart.

They can learn to **sit**.

owner

They like people.

This puppy plays with its **owner**.

Did you find these words?

This puppy plays with its **owner**.

These are Poodle **puppies**!

They can learn to **sit**.

They play with **toys**.

Photo Glossary

 **owner** (OHN-ur): Someone who possesses or has something.

 **puppies** (PUHP-eez): Dogs that are young and not fully grown.

 **sit** (sit): To rest your weight on your hindquarters.

 **toys** (toiz): Objects that someone can play with.

Index

About the Author

Hailey Scragg is a writer from Ohio. She loves all puppies, especially her puppy, Abe! She likes taking him on long walks in the park.

www.rourkeeducationalmedia.com

PHOTO CREDITS: cover: ©Jennifer Stidham, ©manley099 (bone); back cover: ©Naddiya (pattern); back cover (inset), pages 4-5: ©YinYang; pages 2, 3, 14, 15: ©willeecole; pages 6-7: ©Nitik; pages 8-9, 14, 15: ©anetapics; pages 2, 10-11, 14, 15: ©LauraFay; pages 2, 12-13, 14, 15: ©bernardbodo

Edited by: Kim Thompson
Cover and interior design by: Janine Fisher

Library of Congress PCN Data
Poodle Puppies / Hailey Scragg
(Top Puppies)
ISBN 978-1-73162-865-7 (hard cover)(alk. paper)
ISBN 978-1-73162-864-0 (soft cover)
ISBN 978-1-73162-866-4 (e-Book)
ISBN 978-1-73163-342-2 (ePub)
Library of Congress Control Number: 2019945502

Printed in the United States of America,
North Mankato, Minnesota